1. MILITARY PARADE ON THE CASTLE ESPLANADE, c 1930

Published by Hendon Publishing Company Limited, Hendon Mill, Nelson, Lancashire.
Text © Norma Armstrong, 1977
Printed by Fretwell & Brian Ltd., Howden Hall, Silsden, Keighley, Yorks.

Introduction

Edinburgh has a fairly extensive literature, especially in the field of history. Its development from a dark-age fort to a modern city, capital of Scotland and meeting place for the proposed Scottish Assembly, is well known. Many writers have traced the growth of the Old Town, recorded its historic buildings and described the lives of its famous inhabitants.

Excellent source books are available on the history of the New Town also, built to the north of the Old Town in the late 18th century. In modern times, conservation studies show an awareness of the importance of preserving the city's architectural heritage. Most of the villages surrounding the old burgh, now integrated into the modern city, have their historians too, so it is possible to trace their historic buildings and celebrities also.

Few historians have given much thought to the ordinary people of the city, the majority of inhabitants, whose lives and homes have not merited a place in historical record. It is with these *people of Edinburgh* that we are in a modest way concerned. We have attempted to show *Edinburgh as it was* through various aspects of people's lives, the photographs inevitably showing some moment in time in the 19th or 20th centuries, but in the text we have tried to give a glimpse of city life from early times.

Norma Armstrong.

PEOPLE ON THE STREETS

Edinburgh has always been a visually interesting city. Situated between the Pentland Hills and the Firth of Forth, it has a beautiful natural setting. The Old Town was built on a ridge with the Castle at one end and Holyrood Palace and Abbey at the other. Narrow wynds linked the High Street with the Cowgate on the south side, and on the north side led to the Nor' Loch. Early travellers commented on the town's spacious High Street with its mansion houses, some of which still stand today. Behind the facade of the High Street and Lawnmarket, closes lead to attractive courtyards, and on the streets themselves, forestairs, street wells and granite setts add interest for visitors and inhabitants alike.

When the city extended to the north in the late 18th century, a New Town was built, which contrasted greatly with the architecture of the Old Town. Elegant Georgian terraces with spacious houses, gardens and public buildings appeared, which introduced those who moved from the Old Town to a completely new life style. Monuments, statues and fountains were erected to commemorate famous inhabitants and beautify the new streets.

Our photographs give a brief impression of people on the streets and some of the fountains, courts, monuments and bridges, which can be found in many parts of the city.

2. GEORGE STREET AND CORNER OF HANOVER STREET, 1906. As the photographer stood in Hanover Street, he could see that it was ten past four on St. Andrew's Church clock. St. Andrew's was the first church built in the New Town, and George Street one of its three principal streets. The little news vendor is probably selling the first edition of the evening paper, as the ladies glance at Gibb's umbrella shop, with its interesting shop signs.

3

3. SCOTT MONUMENT, PRINCES STREET, 1928. Built in 1846 to commemorate Sir Walter Scott, the Scott Monument is a familiar Edinburgh landmark. This unusual view, taken in November 1928, shows men of the Edinburgh Fire Brigade, under the leadership of Firemaster Methven, carrying out an exercise.

4. ARCHER FOUNTAIN, LEITH, c1895. Built in 1894, with money raised by subscription, the Archer Memorial Fountain stood in Henderson Gardens. Gilbert Archer, a member of a distinguished Leith family had been Registrar for South Leith for many years. It was perhaps appropriate to raise a water fountain to a man whose family had been leaders of the temperance movement in Leith.

5. BAILIE McMORRAN'S HOUSE, RIDDLE'S COURT, c1905. This interesting old house in a courtyard in the Lawnmarket was the home of Bailie McMorran, a member of the Town Council in the 16th century. When he was called out to quell a disturbance in the High School in 1595, he was accidentally shot and killed by one of the boys.

6. CANDLEMAKER ROW AND GREYFRIARS' BOBBY FOUNTAIN, c1930. Taking its name from the Incorporation of Candlemakers, Candlemaker Row joins the Grassmarket and the Cowgate to Bristo. This print shows the ancient hall of the Candlemakers, restored in 1929, with its sculptured stone above the door lintel. The fountain in the foreground commemorates the world-famous Greyfriars' Bobby, the Skye terrier, who kept vigil for fourteen years on his master's grave in the nearby Greyfriars' Churchyard and was eventually buried there himself.

7. ST. JOHN STREET, c1910. St. John Street was reached from the Canongate by the pend shown on No. 50, outlined in white in the background of this photograph. It differed considerably from the other streets of the Old Town, being wide and airy. By the late 19th and early 20th centuries it was occupied by the ordinary people of Edinburgh, but in earlier days had such distinguished inhabitants as Tobias Smollett, Lord Blantyre, the Earls of Dalhousie and Hyndford and James Ballantyne, Sir Walter Scott's friend and publisher.

8. COWGATE AND SOUTH BRIDGE, 1907. In 1785 the foundation stone of an important new bridge was laid, bringing the road from the south. Spanning the valley of the Cowgate, the South Bridge had twenty-two arches, all of which were eventually filled in, except the one seen here over the Cowgate. There is a tradition that in 1815 an illicit still was operating inside one of the arches, reached by an adjacent house. The scene in 1907 seems very respectable with the local children taking a keen interest in the photographer.

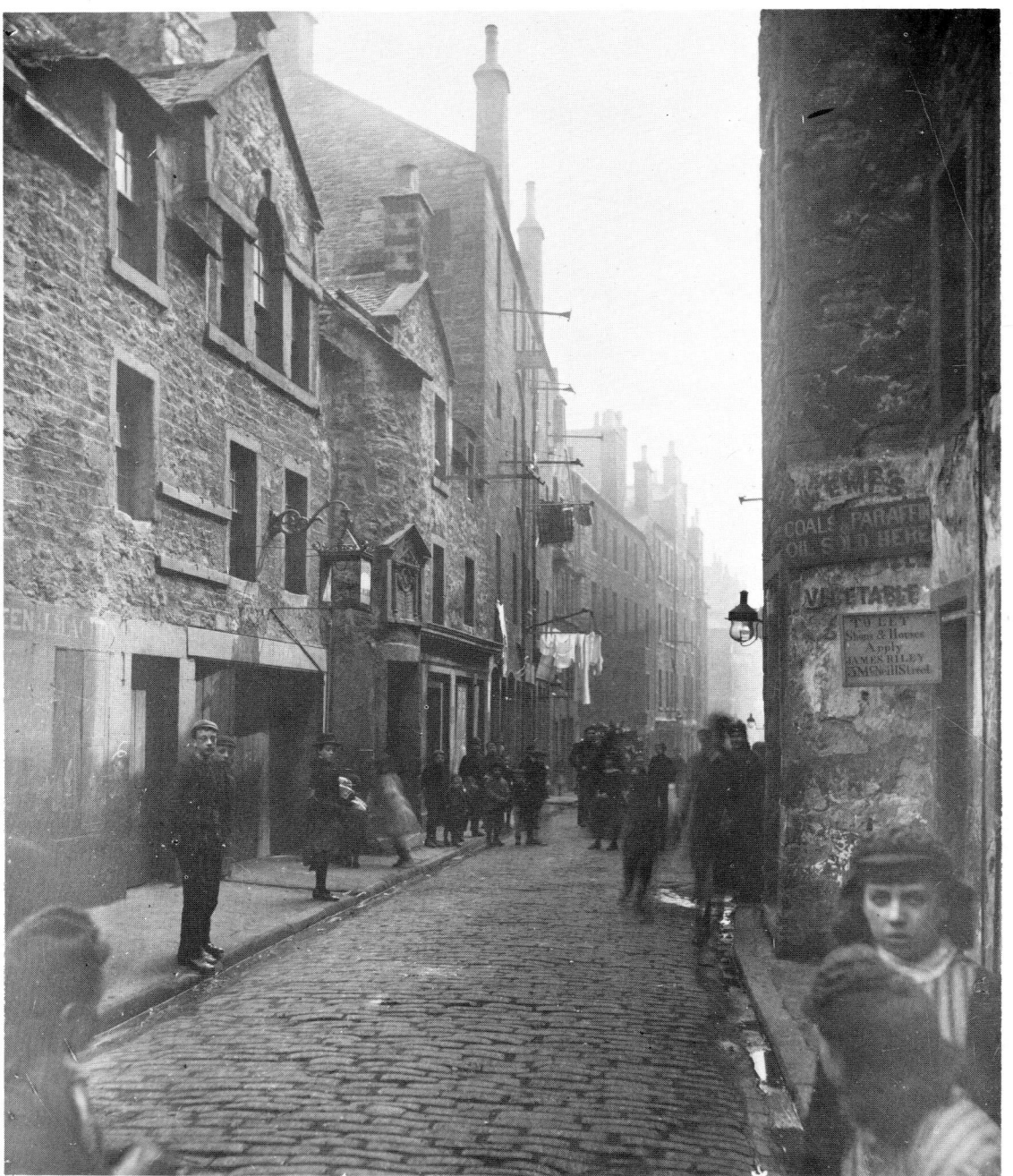

PEOPLE'S HOUSES

During the 19th century many of the social reformers were concerned with housing conditions. The Old Town had certainly deteriorated into a sordid slum with the attendant problems of congestion, poverty and drunkeness. Several factors had led to this situation, mainly the comparatively late extension of the burgh to the north in 1767, when the Old Town was already overcrowded. The high tenement lands had accommodated a good social mix, with the aristocracy, the professions, merchants and working men all living together on different floors of the same tenement. The departure of the well-to-do to the New Town left the working classes in flats, which quickly became overcrowded as they were subdivided.

The earliest dwellings of the ancient town were thatched huts, eventually replaced by wooden-framed mud-plastered houses as the burgh developed. Later in the 16th and 17th centuries, stone town houses and tenements took their place and it was these latter buildings with 18th century additions, that formed the early 19th century slums.

In 1862 with the appointment of the first Medical Officer of Health, improvement schemes were introduced to the Old Town, the closes whitewashed and many unsafe dwellings demolished. With successive boundary extensions, surrounding villages were absorbed into the city, adding more variety to the people's houses, with the distinctive architecture of the fishermen's cottages at Newhaven, miners' houses at Niddrie and Newcraighall, and villas at Morningside and Trinity.

Our photographic selection illustrates a variety of houses, the tenement lands of the Canongate, the congestion of the Potterrow and the tailor's "castle" at St. Leonard's. Huntly House was just one of a number of mansion houses, subdivided into flats and Tron Square, with its balconies, typical of a number of late 19th century improvement schemes.

9. POTTERROW, c1890. Mentioned in records from the 16th century onwards, the Potterrow was an area lying outside the city wall near one of the gates in the wall called the Patterrow Port. It probably tooks its name from the craft of its early inhabitants. In 1673 the Incorporation of Tailors of Portsburgh built their hall, which can be seen with a sculptured stone, bearing the emblems of the craft above the doorway. It obviously contained working class housing in the 1890's but in the 18th century was connected with many people of note, including the Earl of Morton and the Duke of Douglas. Burns was familiar with the area too, because his friend Nancy McLehose (*Clarinda*), lived in General's Entry nearby.

10. TRON SQUARE, c1907. Tron Square was built in one of the improvement schemes, which removed property like that shown in No. 11. Proposed in a report "Dwellings of the Poor", 1894, the site was bounded on the north by the High Street, on the south by the Cowgate, on the east by Blair Street and on the west by Borthwick's Close. The purpose of the scheme was to provide "cheap and convenient houses for the poorest classes" and the flats were planned accordingly, costing £3. 18s. to rent a one-apartment flat and £6. 14s. 4d. for two apartments, per annum.

11. GOLFER'S LAND, CANONGATE, c1910. This close-up view of a Canongate tenement gives a clear picture of Old Town living conditions, at the beginning of the century. Tradition has it that this 17th century land was built by John Patersone, a local shoemaker, who partnered the Duke of York in a game of golf with two English courtiers. With his winnings from the game, Patersone is said to have built this house.

12. LEITH, c1895. Although Leith has been Edinburgh's port since the 12th century, great rivalry has always existed between the two, especially after Leith became a burgh in 1832. In some respects Leith was ahead of Edinburgh but both burghs were alike in the poor housing conditions of the ordinary people.

13. FRIENDS' MEETING HOUSE, PLEASANCE, c1910. This group of housing is unusual, having built into it the burial ground and meeting place of the Society of Friends. The Society was established in Edinburgh in 1655 and its supporters met successively at the West Port, Peebles Wynd and finally the Pleasance. There are several people of note buried here including Priscilla McLaren, who was the sister of the famous reformer John Bright, and the wife of Duncan McLaren, a Lord Provost of Edinburgh.

14. HUNTLY HOUSE, c. 1890. Taking its name from its associations with the Marquis of Huntly in the 17th century, Huntly House stands in Bakehouse Close, in the Canongate. By the late 19th century, it was certainly not a mansion house, but had been divided into apartments for several families, as can be seen by the washing and pulleys hanging from several windows.

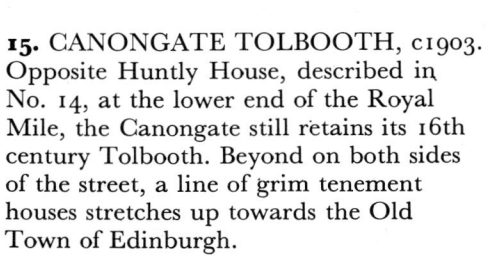

15. CANONGATE TOLBOOTH, c1903. Opposite Huntly House, described in No. 14, at the lower end of the Royal Mile, the Canongate still retains its 16th century Tolbooth. Beyond on both sides of the street, a line of grim tenement houses stretches up towards the Old Town of Edinburgh.

16. CASTLE O' CLOUTS, c1907. A fine example of early 18th century Scots domestic architecture, the Castle o' Clouts stood at the top of St. Leonard's Street. Its strange name was probably an ironic reference to the profession of Hunter, its builder; Hunter being a tailor and *clout* the Scots word for cloth. The part of the building at street level had been a tavern or inn for over 200 years.

PEOPLE AT WORK

The occupations of the people have inevitably been affected by the size of the city, its situation and natural resources. Early inhabitants lived out their lives in wooden huts, tilling the land and tending their cattle. Gradually with the development of the town, trades and crafts were established and merchants were engaged in selling goods. By the 13th century merchant guilds were formed, playing a powerful part in the government of the burgh till 1469, when the Town Council chose its own members. The formation of crafts incorporations such as the hammermen, the baxters (bakers), cordiners (shoemakers), bonnetmakers and dyers indicate the occupations of previous centuries.

Situated between the Pentlands Hills and the Firth of Forth, the old burgh enjoyed the benefits of its proximity to the sea, with fishing villages along the coast and from the 12th century, a harbour at the mouth of its river, the Water of Leith. Leith Harbour gradually became very important to the burgh's economy, trading with the Low Countries, the Baltic and France and eventually with every part of the world.

Early records indicate the presence of mills along the course of the Water of Leith and in the 19th century, paper, flour and snuff mills were flourishing. An excellent water supply led in early times to the brewing industry, still one of the city's most important industries in the 20th century. The 19th century Census Returns make interesting reading, throwing light on the numbers engaged in various occupations and illustrating the needs of the population at that time. Particularly interesting are the returns concerning the occupations of women. Even by 1851 it was clear that the "monstrous regiment" was on the move.

Our choice of photographs illustrates several traditional occupations including the fishwives at Newhaven, the brewery men at Younger's and Oliver and Boyd's printers. Public service occupations are represented by firemen, the cable car repairmen and the police, whilst the coal merchant, the bill poster and the taxi drivers show other aspects of people at work.

17. CABLE CAR REPAIR MEN, c1920. These cable car repair men are working at the junction of Home Street and Gilmore Place and in the background a car from Colinton makes its way towards Tollcross. This route was the last to be served by cable cars, having a three-horse car service until August 1907. The Corporation had completed their programme for the rest of the city by 1903, but took several years to decide whether to install an electric overhead system on this route. They finally adopted the cable system, which opened in April 1908.

13

18. BREWERY WORKERS, YOUNGER'S BREWERY, c 1926. This world-famous brewery was established by William Younger in a "kitchen" brewery in Leith in 1749. After his death his widow and sons all founded separate breweries which were merged in 1819. During the early 19th. century practically every tavern in Edinburgh sold *Younger's Ale*, described as "a potent fluid which almost glued the lips of the drinker together". By the 1840's the firm was exporting all over the world.

19. POLICEMAN, c1860. Although obviously a studio pose, this print is interesting in showing the uniform of an Edinburgh Policeman of the 1860's. The Police force as we understand it today was founded by the Edinburgh Police Act of 1805. Prior to that the duties of "watching" the city had been carried out by the Town Guard, founded in 1690 with the Lord Provost as commander. With the formation of the Police, the Town Guard was gradually reduced and disbanded in 1817.

20. PRINTERS, OLIVER AND BOYD, c1910. In 1778 Thomas Oliver set up business in his own home and in 1807 went into partnership with Boyd, the book-binder. The firm worked from several addresses, moving into Tweeddale Court, the 17th century mansion of the Marquis of Tweeddale, in 1820. During the 19th century many publications appeared with the Oliver and Boyd imprint, particularly editions of Burns, and the works of James Hogg and John Galt. In addition to the interesting old mansion, the court also contains the only remaining sedan-chair shed in the city.

21. FISHWIVES BAITING THE LINES, NEWHAVEN, c1890. Newhaven is one of Edinburgh's villages lying on the shores of the Firth of Forth, famous in the 16th century as the home of the *Great Michael*, the largest ship in the Scottish navy. From earliest times the inhabitants earned their living by fishing, with the women playing an important part in this industry, baiting the lines and selling their wares in the streets of the town.

22. TAXI DRIVERS, JOHN CROALL AND SONS LTD., 22nd JUNE, 1926. Posed with their taxis in Johnson Terrace, just below the Castle, these drivers formed the imposing fleet operated by John Croall. The firm started their service in the early 20th century but were forced to disband their fleet in December 1954, due to economic difficulties.

23. COAL MERCHANT ON PARADE, c 1920. In the 1920's there were at least 134 coal merchants in and around Edinburgh, most of them using Clydesdales and carts for their business. Judging by the immaculate appearance of the coalman, the clean sacks of a coal and the groomed horse, they are about to join a parade, perhaps the same one as the group on No. 63.

24. FIREMEN AT THE CENTRAL FIRE STATION, 30th SEPTEMBER, 1926. Edinburgh has had a succession of distinguished firemasters, including the world-famous James Braidwood. In fact the city had one of the first municipal brigades in the country. This view of the fire station at Lauriston built in 1900, shows men of the brigade at work, under the watchful eye of Firemaster Pordage, who carried on the tradition set by his predecessors.

25. BAKERS, c1930. The trade of baker stretches far back in Edinburgh history. In the 16th century we find proclamations instructing the baxters (as the craft was called then) neither to burn nor water their bread, but to mark it with the correct weight and keep to the statutory size and price. This photograph shows some interesting detail in the work of a 20th century baker. In the foreground are swiss rolls, newly baked and spread with jam. Behind, we can see the machines used for cutting dough.

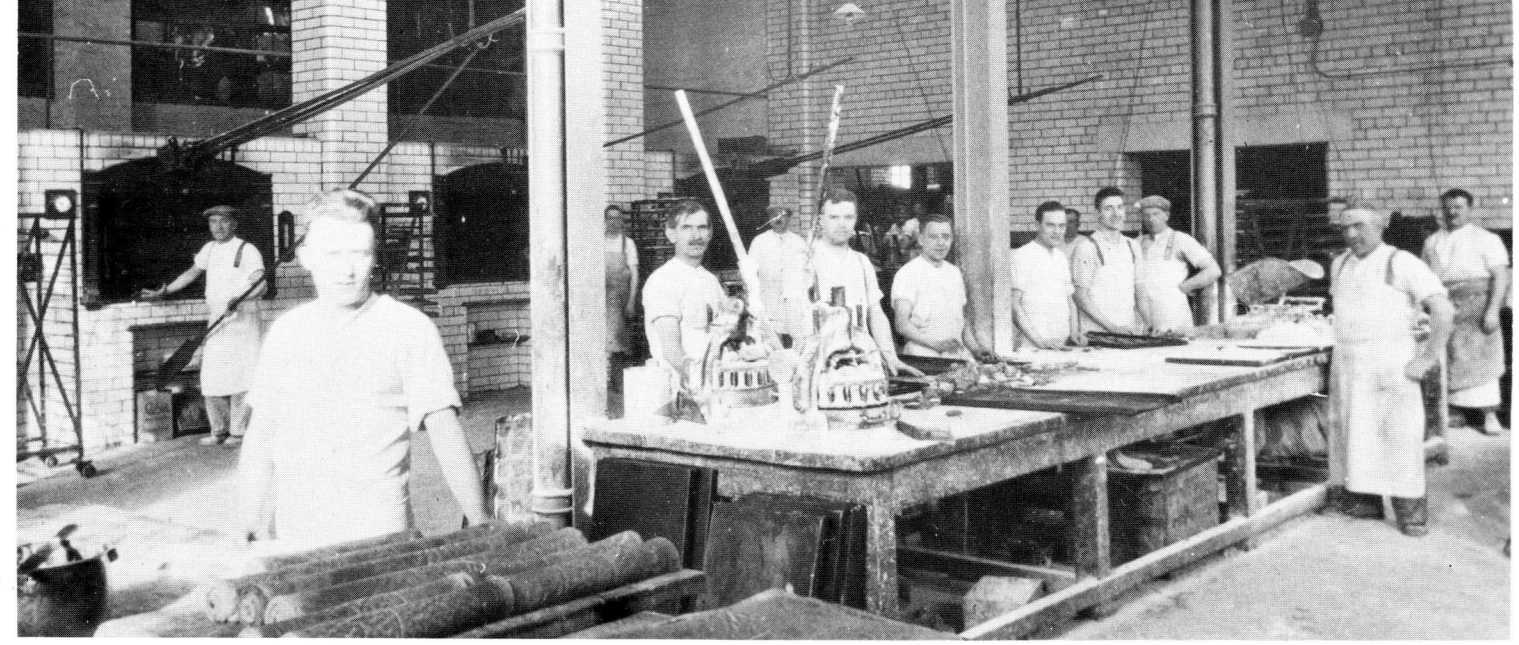

26. BILL POSTER AT CORSTORPHINE STATION, 1926.
There must have been a fair number of bill posters at work in the city in the 1920's judging by the large number of bill boardings to be found in photographs of the period. This photograph taken in January 1926 (if the bill for the revue at the Empire Theatre is to be believed) shows a typical group of adverts outside Corstorphine Station. At this period the suburban railway was still very much in use. Opened in 1884 it incorporated an inner circle, an outer circle and Leith branch line, with stations conveniently placed throughout the city. Incredible as it seems, in the early days the round trip was 3d return and trains ran from 5.30 am – 11 pm daily.

PEOPLE AT LEISURE

Our ancestors did not have our preoccupation with leisure, mainly because long working hours left little time or inclination for recreation. Before the Reformation, feast days and Sundays were the only days of rest and after 1560, with the abolition of feast days, only Sundays remained. It was little wonder that ministers complained that their congregations were not observing the Sabbath and that legislation was necessary to cause people to do so. These Acts of Parliament forbidding certain amusements on the Sabbath, indicate that there was a fair choice of pastimes, namely golf, archery, rowbowls (bowls), penny-stane (quoits) and catchpel (tennis) among others. The Minutes of the Town Council of the 16th century also indicate that there were performances of players, musicians and tight-rope dancers.

During the 18th century the popularity of plays and concerts increased and Edinburgh had its first specially designed theatre, thanks to Allan Ramsay, in 1736. By the late 19th century the number of sports pastimes had grown and concerts and the theatre were well established leisure activities, and as working hours decreased, more people had time to participate in them. Our photographs illustrate a selection of sports, listening to the band, some street entertainers and the pleasures of sunbathing at Portobello, all of which may seem unsophisticated compared with present standards.

27. CYCLING IN FISHWIVES' CAUSEWAY, c1910. The two young cyclists would have every opportunity to practise in this quiet byroad. The Fishwives' Causeway follows the line of an old Roman road and takes its name from the fishwives, who walked with their creels on their backs, from the fishing village of Fisherrow, to sell their fish in the city. In the background, the bottlework's chimneys and brickwork's kilns are reminders of the industries in Portobello nearby.

28. BOWLING, EAST MEADOWS, 1908. South of the Castle there was a large expanse of water called the Burgh Loch, which was partially drained in the 17th century. During the 18th century the draining was completed and in 1860 the Town Council accepted estimates for laying out walks and a bowling green. This area, near the centre of the town, became popular for sport, as is indicated in a report of 1908, in which it is noted that 25,635 players had used the two bowling greens on the East Meadows, during that year.

29. GOLF, MORTONHALL GOLF COURSE, 1892. Golf has been a popular sport in Scotland for many centuries, so it is not surprising that there are many courses in and around the city. Mortonhall Golf Course, seen here, was laid out as a 9 hole course, on the steep southern slopes of the Braid Hills in 1892. So hilly was the course that the second hole was nicknamed *Khyber*.

30. BOATING AT CRAMOND, c1910. The village of Cramond takes its name from *Caer-Amon*, the fort on the River Almond, commemorating the site of an important Roman station. When the rower in the foreground stepped ashore, he was probably not aware he was following the footsteps of the Emperor Septimus Severus, who landed there in 208 AD for a tour of Scotland. During the 18th and early 19th centuries a flourishing iron industry was carried on at the nearby mills.

31. PORTOBELLO BEACH AND PIER, c1910. In the early 20th century Portobello was a popular holiday resort with its stretch of beach, donkeys, pier and pavilion. Nearby the Marine Gardens, opened in 1910, provided additional entertainment with a ballroom, concert hall, amusement court and sports area. Admission to the Marine Gardens, including a return rail fare to Waverley Station, was only 7d. With the further attraction of Forth steamers calling at the pier, the holidaymaker had all he could desire.

32. HERBERT PARKIN, THE FIDDLER ENTERTAINING IN THE GRASSMARKET, c1980. Herbert Parkin was one of a number of street characters familiar in Edinburgh at the turn of the century. He was well-known particularly in the Bruntsfield, Morningside and Braid districts of the city with his ginger beard, his fiddle and his spaniel at his heels. It was said that he had played in the Brighton Theatre Orchestra. Certainly he composed several pieces which were published by a local publisher and sold at 1d. each. He was also a regular performer at "Go-As-You-Please" competitions in the Star Picture House and won the 10/- prize on occasion.

33. DANCING IN THE STREETS, NEW-CRAIGHALL, 1926. During the General Strike there was a most unusual form of entertainment at Newcraighall, a mining village on the outskirts of Edinburgh. Two local men, Messrs. Macmillan and Pat Brogan, with the accompaniment of a melodion provided tap dancing in the streets.

34. SKATING ON DUDDINGSTON LOCH, c1900. In the early part of this century, with very severe winters it was quite common to be able to skate on local lochs. Duddingston Loch is one of three in Holyrood Park, a large natural park near the centre of the city. In the background, Duddingston Village and its church can be seen on the hill.

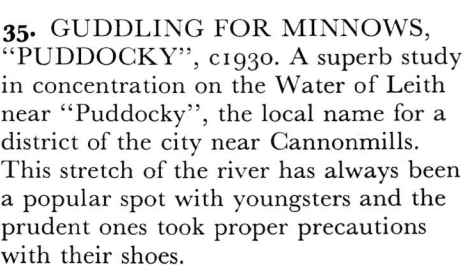

35. GUDDLING FOR MINNOWS, "PUDDOCKY", c1930. A superb study in concentration on the Water of Leith near "Puddocky", the local name for a district of the city near Cannonmills. This stretch of the river has always been a popular spot with youngsters and the prudent ones took proper precautions with their shoes.

36. STOCKING THE WATER OF LEITH, 1922. Edinburgh's river, the Water of Leith has always played an important part in the life of the city. From earliest times there are records of mills along its course and the Port of Leith was built at the mouth of the river. Besides providing industries it also provided sport, and a regular annual occurence was the stocking of the river with trout by the Honorary Bailiffs. At the period of this stocking ceremony, seen near St. Bernard's Well, just below the Dean Village, fishing was free, but in 1939 permits cost 1/- each.

37. LISTENING TO THE BAND, PRINCES STREET GARDENS, c1905. A popular pastime in Edinburgh was listening to military bands and ten of the public parks had bandstands. The most popular of these were Portobello and Princes Street Gardens. The Ross Bandstand drew the largest crowds. Beautifully situated in Princes Street Gardens, the bandstand normally presented twenty-six concerts in a season.

PEOPLE ON THE MOVE

Without a doubt, the earliest people of Edinburgh would travel on foot, using horses for drawing loads and for longer journeys. During the 17th century occasional stage coaches ran between Edinburgh and Leith and Edinburgh and London. By the 18th century these services were well established, the London journey taking 10 days in summer and 12 in winter.

Special coaches also operated during the summer from the city to the nearby holiday resorts of Morningside, Corstorphine and Portobello, which were the forerunners of the regular horse-bus services of the 1870's. In 1871, horse-trams were introduced, which by 1874 required a fleet of 37 tramway cars and 300 horses to serve the city. Horse power was superceded by 1888 by cable trams and eventually in 1922, an electric tramway system was introduced.

For those 17th century inhabitants who did not wish to dirty their feet on the streets of the Old Town, an alternative was offered in 1687 with the introduction of the first sedan chair service. So popular was this service that the 6 original chairs were increased to 90 by 1738. The large number of chairs led to the city's first parking restriction in 1723, when anyone parking outwith the designated "chair park" at the Tron, was fined 2/6d.

Railways were introduced in 1826 with the construction of the Edinburgh and Dalkeith Railway. Successive local lines followed in the 1830's and 1840's and with the completion of the final section of the Caledonian Railway in 1848, the west coast route to London was inaugurated with a running time of 12 hours.

An alternative to road travel to Glasgow had been offered in 1822 with the opening of the Union Canal, with a modest fare of 2/-, first cabin or 1/4d., second cabin. The opening of the railways overshadowed this form of transport and the canal was sold to the Edinburgh and Glasgow Railway Company in 1848.

Until the opening of the Forth Rail Bridge in 1890, it was necessary for a traveller to Fife and the north to cross the Forth by ferry at Leith, Granton or Queensferry. By 1826 regular ferries plied in the Forth, the *Dumbarton Castle, the Thane of Fife* and the *Willie Muir* being household words with the people of Edinburgh.

Our photographs show some of the ways that people could go on the move, either within the city itself or farther afield.

38. SCOTTISH MOTOR TRACTION BUS AT THE MOUND, 30th JANUARY 1931. Founded in 1905, the Scottish Motor Traction Company started services on 1st January, 1906. Eventually taken over by the British Transport Commission and called Scottish Omnibuses Ltd., this Company developed travel between Edinburgh and surrounding towns and villages. This interesting photograph, taken at the foot of the Mound on Princes Street, shows the uniform and ticket machine of a conductor in the 1930's. A close examination shows it to be an experimental bus, fitted with a National Cash Register till.

39. LEITH SHORE AND BERNARD STREET BRIDGE, 1922. This unusual view of the Shore and Bernard Street Bridge illustrates several forms of transport. Obviously in the 1920's small boats and even larger ships still tied up at the quayside. Two motor cars are in sight, a bus is about to turn from the Shore into Bernard Street and an electric tram has just left the Bridge (Leith converted straight from horse cars to electric traction between 1904 and 1905).

40. TAXI, c 1910. This form of transport would not be generally used by the people of Edinburgh, as it was expensive to hire at 1/- for the first mile and 2d for every additional quarter mile. Seen here at the side of the Royal Scottish Academy, facing the Old Town, with East Princes Street Gardens and the Christopher North monument in the background, this particular model looks very similar to the Argyll taxi produced between 1905 and 1910.

41. HORSE-BUS AT FOUNTAINBRIDGE, c1900. This interesting photograph, taken on the drawbridge at Fountainbridge depicts two forms of transport. The horse-bus travelling between Gorgie and Tollcross is quite obvious. Not so obvious, below the bridge, is the Union Canal which, linked Edinburgh with the Forth and Clyde Canal. From the nearby terminal at Port Hopetoun it was possible to "make swift passage" to Glasgow at nine miles per hour.

42. EDINBURGH CORPORATION BUSES, ANNANDALE STREET, c1929. The first motor bus service in the city was a private one started in May 1898 (over a year before they were introduced in London). Prior to 1914, six buses were operated by the Edinburgh District Tramways Company on behalf of Edinburgh Corporation and after the Great War, in December 1919, the Corporation inaugurated its own services with the purchase of 12 buses, used to develop routes in areas not served by trams. Taken in Annandale Street near the Central Garage, bought by the Corporation in 1926, this photograph shows the A.E.C.'s of the early fleet and the uniforms of both conductors and drivers.

43. TRAFFIC JAM, FOUNTAINBRIDGE, c1910. Taken at the corner of Fountainbridge and Earl Grey Street, this photograph shows some congestion with one of the cable fleet, run by Edinburgh and District Tramways Company, on behalf of Edinburgh Corporation. Conversion from horse, to cable trams began in 1893 and was completed on all routes, except for Colinton, by 1903. This particular tram ran from Abbeyhill via Princes Street and Tollcross, to Morningside. Covering 36 miles of track and operating 14 main cables, from 4 power stations, the Edinburgh cable tramway system was one of the largest in the world.

44. COAL WHARF, UNION CANAL, c1912. Opened in 1822 the Union Canal joined the Forth and Clyde Canal at Camelon, linking Edinburgh with Glasgow. In its early days 8 passenger boats regularly plied between Edinburgh and Glasgow each week-day. The opening of the Edinburgh and Glasgow Railway in 1842 put an end to passenger traffic but 32 barges continued to carry coal until about 1921.

45. HORSE-TRAM ON THE SOUTH BRIDGE. c1890. Taken outside the Old Quad of Edinburgh University on the South Bridge, this photograph shows that "horse" power was still very important. The Edinburgh Street Tramways Company had started their services in 1871 and by 1874 were operating 37 tramway cars and 300 horses. Bound for Newington from the G.P.O., this tram could take up to 30 passengers.

46. ELECTRIC TRAM, PORTOBELLO POWER STATION, 1954. Taken opposite Portobello Power Station, the 21 tram ran between Levenhall and the G.P.O. Edinburgh began its conversion from cable to electric trams in 1922 and by 1954 this particular tram was in its last year of service, the route being served by buses from November of that year. Opened in 1923 by George V, the Power Station had the highest chimney in Scotland.

PEOPLE SHOPPING

Although the very earliest people of Edinburgh probably were mainly occupied on the land, it would soon become necessary to make and sell goods to the increasing population of the expanding burgh. Documents of the 14th century indicate that Edinburgh was by then a fair-sized town with mills and a port at Leith. One charter mentions the building of a tron for weighing goods and another, referring to the building of the first Tolbooth, indicates that there was already a market place. An Act of the Town Council of 1583 lists the goods sold by merchant burgesses, namely linen, frieze, Yorkshire cloth, oil, soap, butter, fruit, eggs, figs, raisins, fish and vinegar. More exotic goods such as wine, wax, spices, silks, cloths of gold, silver and fine foreign woollens were sold by Guild Brethren. The regular trade of the town was carried on in booths or houses, mainly clustered around St. Giles, under the galleries of the High Street houses or in the Cowgate.

The earliest known situation of the markets is recorded in a letter of James III in 1477, with hay, straw and grass in the Cowgate, meat round the Tron and poultry by the Markat Cross. There were also specified weekly market days with people travelling long distances to buy and sell in the town, as is shown by letters sent to Ayr, Glasgow, Selkirk and Jedburgh in 1592, reporting a change of market day.

Over the years the markets had many changes of position but modern street names, such as Lawnmarket, Grassmarket, Fishmarket Close and Fleshmarket Close, mark their latest sites. The most famous of the covered markets was the fruit and vegetable market, which stood near the Waverley Bridge. Originally an open market it was roofed over in 1877 and often used as a meeting place for large gatherings.

With the development of the town the old booths and markets disappeared and shops appeared throughout the High Street area. This and the North and South Bridges were popular shopping districts. Initially the New Town was planned purely for housing but gradually shops moved in there too and Princes Street has become a world-famous shopping street.

The photographs show a range of shops from the splendid Princess Street grocer to the more humble premises in the Canongate and the Pleasance.

47. (left) & **48.** (above) WAVERLEY MARKET, c 1905. Over the years the city's fruit and vegetable market had several sites, the best known being the Waverley Market, opened in 1869. At first an open market, it was roofed over with an ornamental garden in 1877. The two views show the approach to the market, with its garden roof and the interior in use as a market. Being such a large hall, it was occasionally used for public meetings, circuses, and carnivals. After the removal of the vegetable market in the 1930's, the building was used for a variety of public events and finally demolished in 1973.

49 & 50. BOVRIL AT CANONGATE, 1935. On a first glance there might seem to be no connection between a florist's shop in the Canongate and an early *Bovril* delivery van. It was however in the basement of this shop, when occupied by a butcher, that *Bovril* was invented. Robert Lawson Johnston served his apprenticeship with his uncle, who had a butcher's shop at 180 Canongate. Eventually Robert took over the business which he managed between 1862 and 1889. Some time during this period he experimented with *Johnston's Beef Fluid* and opened a small factory in Holyrood Square. He subsequently emigrated to Canada and his invention became the world famous *Bovril*.

51. SHOPS AT ROYAL EXCHANGE, c 1880. A handsome building with a piazza, the Royal Exchange was completed in 1761. Unfortunately the local merchants preferred to continue their business transactions at their traditional place at the Mercat Cross, so the Royal Exchange was eventually taken over in 1811 as the meeting place for the Town Council. During the late 19th century six shops were built into the fine arcaded entrance, completely spoiling the facade. The open arch gives some idea of the size of the shops, which look as if they had an upper floor, judging by the diced pattern of top hat boxes stored in G. Hardie the hatters.

52. R. and T. GIBSON, PRINCES STREET, 1935. A splendid example of a high class family grocer, R. & T. Gibson opened in 98 Princes Street in 1848. They moved to new premises in 1859 at 95 Princes Street, which were extended through to Frederick Street in 1889. The firm sold out in 1951 to Littlewood's who still occupy the premises. R. & T. Gibson typifies a lost era in shopping, where the seated customer received courteous personal attention, buying York ham and chocolate dragees at 1/9d and 2/- per pound, respectively.

53. STOBO TAYLOR'S, PLEASANCE, 1st OCTOBER, 1928. When he retired from business in 1953, Robert Stobo Taylor recalled his 57 years service to the public in the Old Town. Starting as an apprentice of 20, he spoke of the days when there were five drapers in this area, all opening till 11 o'clock on a Saturday night and offering a shop girl 4/– per week in wages.

54. ADAIR & CO., 74-75 SOUTH BRIDGE, 1902. Locally known as "the Bridges", the North and South Bridges were popular shopping areas, with Adair & Co. a well established firm. Perhaps the most interesting detail in this advert is the cost of various items of clothing. Note the prudent Scots "Rise and Fall" which would allow the garments to be lengthened as the child grew.

55. RENTON'S PRINCES STREET, c 1929. Renton's set up in business on the North Bridge in 1805, moving to 14 Princes Street in 1840. They were one of the first firms to move into the New Town, and the first to fit plate-glass windows nearly to ground level. In 1908 they bought the property then occupied by Cranston and Elliot at 37-38 Princes Street, extending in the 1920's to the adjacent building belonging to the Sun Insurance Company. This building, 38-42 Princes Street, the lower one in the photograph, was one of the oldest in the street, having been one of the original Georgian houses. Renton's disappeared in 1935 when their property was acquired by C. & A. Modes.

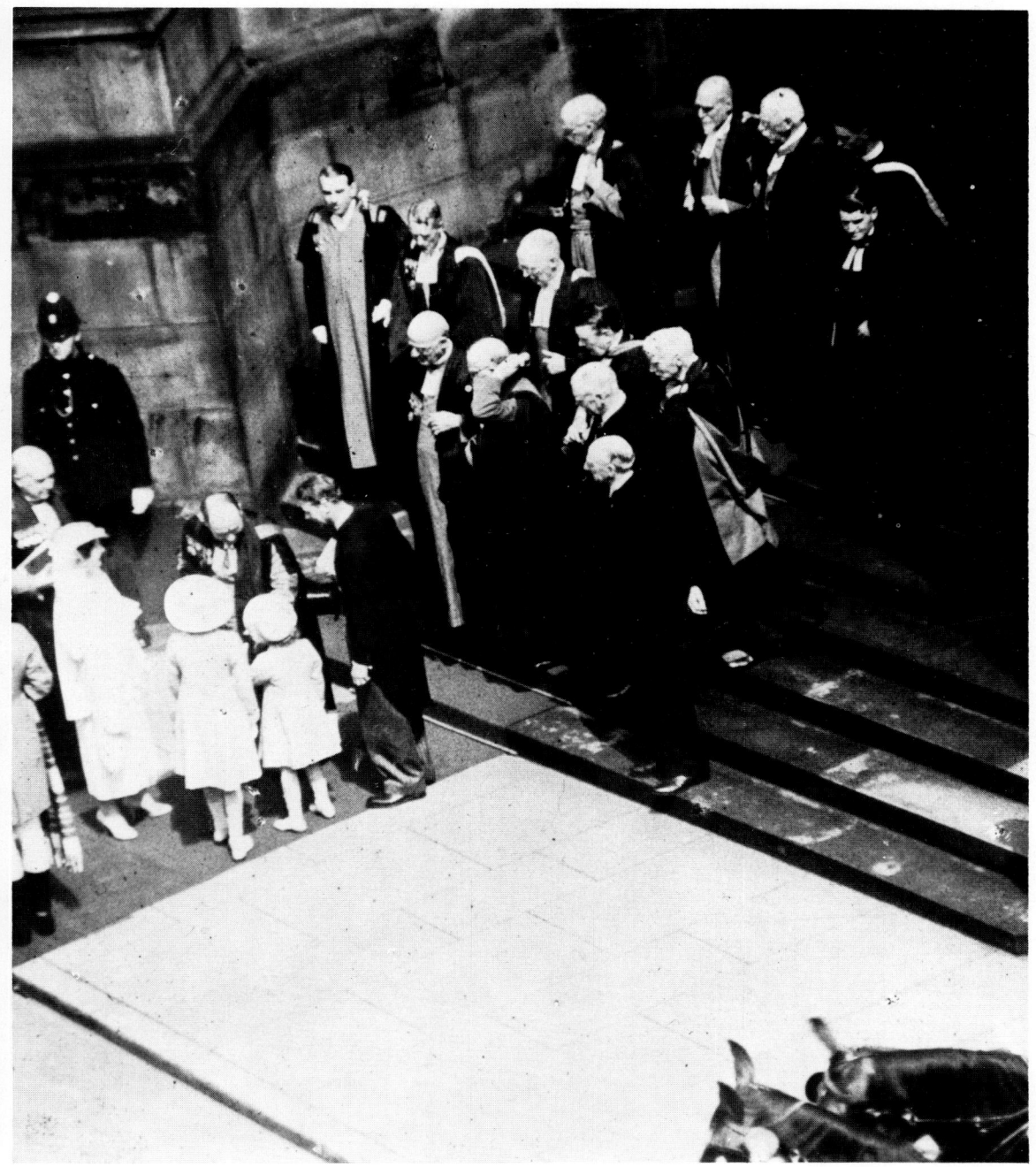

PEOPLE AND SPECIAL OCCASIONS

As inhabitants of the capital of Scotland, the people of Edinburgh were inevitably spectators and often participants at the important events of Scottish history, many of these events connected with warfare or royalty, or sometimes with both. From the dark ages onwards, a succession of tribes including the Celts, the Angles and the Scots had captured the fortress at Edinburgh. By the 14th century, Scotland was engaged in the Wars of Independence from England and many Scottish castles including Edinburgh were occupied by English troops.

During the 16th century the two great disasters of Flodden and the Earl of Hertford's invasion had a devastating effect on the lives of the ordinary people of the burgh. Many Edinburgh women were widowed by the Battle of Flodden and Hertford burnt both the Castle and the Abbey of Holyrood. The successive occupation of the town by Cromwell and his troops in the 17th century, and Prince Charles Edward Stuart and the Jacobite Army in 1745 also disrupted the lives of the ordinary people. After the failure of the '45 no more invading troops passed through the Edinburgh streets, though unfortunately the people were still involved in wars.

After Edinburgh became capital of Scotland in the 14th century, the Abbey of Holyrood was used for royal ceremonies of every kind. From that time therefore the people were familiar with processions and pageants which must have added colour to their lives. One can imagine the spectacle of Mary, Queen of Scots riding in procession from Leith to Edinburgh in 1561, and the excitement of the royal visits of George IV in 1822 and Queen Victoria in 1842.

The photographs show that right into the 20th century, royal visits were still special occasions for the people and that pageants and exhibitions could still draw the crowds.

56. GEORGE VI AND QUEEN ELIZABETH, 1937. After the Coronation in 1937, the King and Queen, with Princess Elizabeth and Princess Margaret, paid a state visit to Scotland. During this Coronation visit, which lasted from the 5th - 12th July, with processions and a court at Holyroodhouse, the people of Edinburgh had every opportunity to see the new Royal family. Here we see them chatting to the clergy after morning service at St. Giles Cathedral on Sunday, 11th July.

57. PROCLAMATION AT THE MERCAT CROSS, 1898.
A focal point in Scottish burgh life, the Mercat Cross in
Edinburgh was a meeting place for merchants and others with
business to transact. The Lord Lyon, accompanied by his heralds
and pursuivants also made proclamations at the Cross.

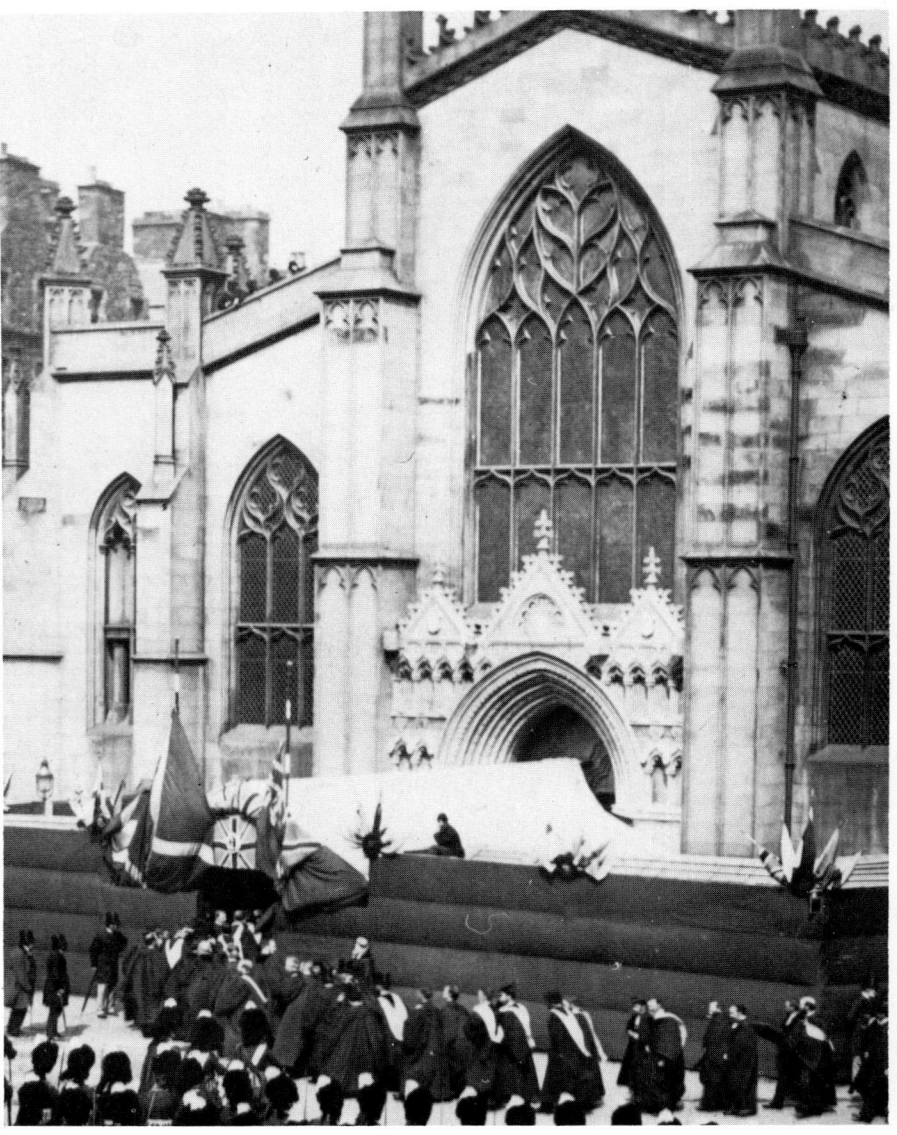

58. RE-OPENING OF ST. GILES CATHEDRAL, 23rd MAY,
1883. An important ecclesiastical event took place in May 1883
with the re-opening of St. Giles, (founded in the 9th century)
after extensive restoration paid for by William Chambers the
publisher.

59. GEORGE V AND QUEEN MARY, 1911. These elaborate decorations were set up at the West End of Princes Street when George V and Queen Mary visited the city, accompanied by the Price of Wales and Princess Mary. During a full programme the King was present at the dedication ceremony of the new Thistle Chapel in St. Giles Cathedral and laid the foundation stone of the Usher Hall.

6o. SCOTTISH NATIONAL EXHIBITION, 1908. Held at Saughton, this exhibition set out to illustrate the achievements of Scotland in industry, science and art, although it included Japanese and Italian sections, and an oriental pavilion. This view shows the throng around the bandstand and Van Houten's pavilion in the background.

61. INTERNATIONAL FORESTRY EXHIBITION, 29th AUGUST, 1884. One of the most interesting exhibits at this exhibition, held in the grounds of Donaldson's Hospital, was an electric railway. Designed by an eccentric gentleman called Henry Bock Binko, the railway carried many distinguished visitors including Mr. and Mrs. Gladstone who are seen here in the *Alexandra Car*.

62. INTERNATIONAL EXHIBITION OF INDUSTRY, SCIENCE AND ARTS, 1886. This spectacular exhibition laid out on the Meadows, with its main entrance in Melville Drive at Brougham Place, covered seven acres. In addition to pavilions for industry and science, it had extensive art galleries, all of which were much admired by its many visitors, including Queen Victoria, the Prince and Princess of Wales and Mr. & Mrs. Gladstone. Particularly popular with the local people were the *Old Edinburgh Street,* a scale reconstruction of a street in the Old Town, the performances of the military bands and the illuminations provided by 1200 coloured lights.

63. LEITH HOSPITAL PAGEANT, c 1920. Two annual events which invariably drew large crowds, were the Royal Infirmary and Leith Hospital Pageants. Most of the principal shops and organisations sent floats and dressed vehicles to the parades. This cart is probably ready to take part in the Leith Hospital Pageant with its well-groomed Clydesdale, model house and chimney sweep. The parade served two purposes, helping to collect money for the hospital and giving the participants free publicity.